Why Science Matters

Exploring the Solar System

John Farndon

Heinemann
LIBRARY

www.heinemann.co.uk/library
Visit our website to find out more information about **Heinemann Library** books.

To order:

 Phone 44 (0) 1865 888066

 Send a fax to 44 (0) 1865 314091

 Visit the Heinemann Bookshop at www.heinemann.co.uk/library to browse our catalogue and order online.

Heinemann Library is an imprint of Capstone Global Library Limited, a company incorporated in England and Wales having its registered office at 7 Pilgrim Street, London, EC4V 6LB – Registered company number: 6695582

"Heinemann" is a registered trademark of Pearson Education Limited, under licence to Capstone Global Library Limited

Edited by Pollyanna Poulter and Rebecca Vickers
Designed by Steven Mead and Q2A Creative Solutions
Original illustrations © Capstone Global Library Limited by Gordon Hurden
Picture research by Ruth Blair
Production by Victoria Fitzgerald
Originated by Steve Walker, Capstone Global Library Ltd
Printed and bound in China by Leo Paper Group.

ISBN 978 0 431040 91 2 (hardback)
13 12 11 10 09
10 9 8 7 6 5 4 3 2 1

British Library Cataloguing-in-Publication Data

Farndon, John
Exploring the solar system. - (Why science matters)
1. Outer space - Exploration - Juvenile literature
2. Solar system - Juvenile literature
I. Title
629.4'1
A full catalogue record for this book is available from the British Library.

Acknowledgements
We would like to thank the following for permission to reproduce photographs: © Alamy pp. **9** (Laurence Delderfield), **10** (Bruno Sinnah), **18** (Blickwinkel), **23** (Tim Gartside), **30** (The Print Collector), **31** (Malcolm Park astronomy images), **34** (Trip), **38** (J Marshall – Tribaleye Images), **39** (NASA Images), **45** (Jupiterimages/Brand X); © Corbis pp. **4** (Tim Kiusalaas), **7** (Jim Sugar), **16** (NASA/Roger Ressmeyer), **24** (Michael Busselle), **36** (Ali Jarekji/Reuters); © Getty Images pp. **37** (Taxi), **42** (NASA/JPL/AFP); © Istockphoto background images and design features; © Science Photo Library pp. **11** (Andrew Brookes, National Physical Laboratory), **17** (Chris Butler), **21** (Center for Space Research/NASA), **22** (Stephen & Donna O'Meara), **26** (Detlev Van Ravenswaay), **32**, **33**, **44**, and **46** (NASA), **35** (NASA/JPL/U. Arizona), **40** (European Space Agency).

Cover photograph of an Exploration Rover on Mars reproduced with permission of © Science Photo Library/NASA.

We would like to thank Geza Gyuk for his invaluable help in the preparation of this book.

Every effort has been made to contact copyright holders of material reproduced in this book. Any omissions will be rectified in subsequent printings if notice is given to the Publishers.

Disclaimer

Contents

Some words are printed in bold, **like this**. You can find out what they mean in the glossary.

Earth in its place

Earth is far from alone in space. Not only is there the Moon to keep it company, but seven other worlds or **planets**, all circling the Sun like Earth. Many planets have their own moons. In between and beyond the planets are tiny chunks of rock and ice called **asteroids** and **dwarf planets**, as well as chunks of dust and ice called comets. Together, the Sun and everything that circles it is called the **solar** system.

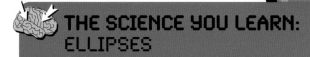

THE SCIENCE YOU LEARN: ELLIPSES

It was originally thought that planets travelled round the Sun in a perfect circle. Then Johannes Kepler (1571–1630) worked out that they move in an ellipse. An ellipse is like a circle with the centre stretched out between two points, known as foci.

Until just over 200 years ago, only five planets besides Earth were known: Mercury, Mars, Venus, Jupiter, and Saturn. Only these planets can be seen with the naked eye. But powerful telescopes revealed two more: first Uranus (in 1781), then Neptune (in 1846). A distant ninth was spotted and named Pluto in 1930, but **astronomers** now say it is too small to be called a planet. This is because they now believe there may be up to 200 dwarf planets as big as Pluto, some of which are likely to be **plutoids**.

The solar system is at least 20 billion km (12 billion miles) across. If Earth were the size of a grain of salt, the solar system would be the size of a sports stadium!

Exploring the solar system

We now know that the solar system is just a tiny island in the huge expanse of the universe – and that there may be billions of similar systems circling stars out in space. Yet it is a vast place and our exploration of it is only just beginning. Until recently, the only way to find out about space was by peering through telescopes. But now we can explore it more closely by sending up spacecraft. Unmanned space probes have now visited all the planets, and a few have even touched down on the surface of Mars. Human beings have also actually set foot on the Moon several times.

Earth moves

When astronomers in ancient times looked at the night sky they noticed something strange. While most stars move slowly through the sky in a fixed pattern, the five planets move differently, shifting a little further eastwards against the background of stars each night. Astronomers assumed that Earth was fixed in place. If so, most of this movement could be explained simply by imagining the planets circling Earth, much closer than the stars. Yet, occasionally, planets loop back and travel westwards for a few months before resuming their eastward journey. Astronomers now call this brief reverse **retrograde motion**, but the ancient astronomers found it hard to explain. It couldn't be that the planets were just stopping and going backwards! Then in the early 1500s, Copernicus (1473–1543) realized that Earth is actually moving around the Sun as well. If so, retrograde motion is easy to explain. It's simply our view from Earth of a faster-moving planet overtaking us (as those closer to the Sun do), or our view from Earth of Earth overtaking a slower-moving planet (like those further from the Sun).

30/5
19/6
27/10
16/11
26/11
17/9
29/7

As they orbit the Sun, faster-orbiting planets overtake Earth, while slower-orbiting planets are overtaken. For a few months, they appear to loop through the night sky. This is retrograde motion.

Holding it all together

The astonishing thing about the solar system is that the planets and everything else have been circling round the Sun now for a very long time – and show no signs of stopping. Earth alone has journeyed round the Sun over 4 billion times! It is not just Earth and the planets that seem to circle. Nearly every object in space travels in paths called **orbits**.

The key to orbits is **gravity** and **momentum**. Gravity is the force that makes objects fall and keeps them on the ground. It also controls all the movement of the stars and planets. In fact, gravity is the force that pulls every single bit of matter in the universe towards every other bit. The bigger and heavier something is, and the closer it is, the stronger gravity pulls. The Sun's **mass** is so vast that its gravitational pull is enough to hold the entire solar system together.

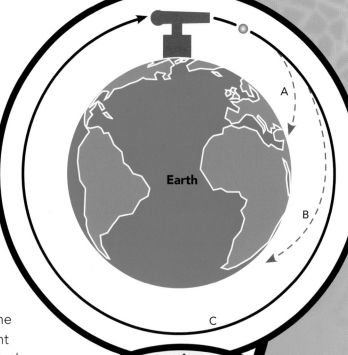

Earth

In the 1600s, Isaac Newton explained orbits using an imaginary giant cannon. His idea was that if a cannonball were fired fast enough it would have enough momentum to fly on and on around Earth, without being pulled down by gravity. If a slow-fired cannonball was released (as shown by paths A and B) it would soon fall as its momentum is overcome by gravity. But if it was fired fast enough, its momentum would be so great that gravity would never quite be enough to bring it down and it would go on circling the Earth in an orbit (as in path C).

CUTTING EDGE: REVERSING GRAVITY

In recent years, scientists have been wondering if they can counteract or reverse gravity to stop things falling. In 1997, British and Dutch scientists made a frog float in mid-air using powerful magnets to repel atoms in the frog's body. Now scientists at places such as Boeing, NASA, and the European Space Agency are trying to develop anti-gravity devices to make much larger objects hover in the air. These devices use **superconducting magnets**. The highly disputed results seem to show gravity being cancelled out on a larger scale. This means that objects lose the **weight** that normally pulls them down.

Staying moving

Momentum, or as scientists more commonly call it, **inertia**, is the tendency for things to keep moving in a straight line (or stay still), unless they are forcibly stopped (or started). It is the planets' momentum that keeps them moving. But momentum alone would send them off on a straight path. It is gravity that pulls them into a roughly circular orbit.

In fact, gravity and momentum are in perfect balance. If gravity were stronger, the planets would spiral towards the Sun. If it were weaker, then planets would fly off into space. Everything that orbits in space, from a planet to an artificial satellite, is held in this perfect balance between gravity and momentum.

A fast-moving spacecraft counteracts the effects of gravity causing anything onboard that is not fixed down to float. →

 THE SCIENCE YOU LEARN: MASS AND WEIGHT

When ordinary people talk about how heavy something is, they often talk about its great weight. Scientists, however, talk instead about an object's mass, which is basically how much matter it contains. Weight, for scientists, is something different; it is the force with which gravity is pulling on the object.

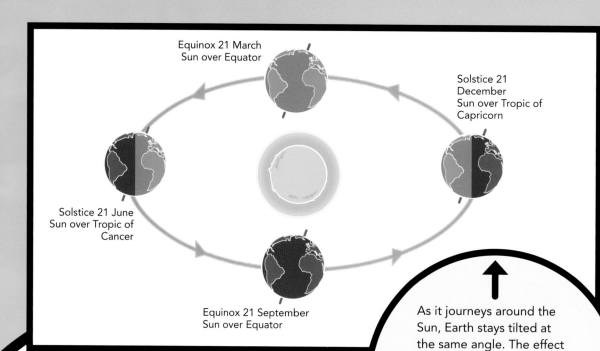

Equinox 21 March
Sun over Equator

Solstice 21
December
Sun over Tropic of
Capricorn

Solstice 21 June
Sun over Tropic of
Cancer

Equinox 21 September
Sun over Equator

As it journeys around the
Sun, Earth stays tilted at
the same angle. The effect
is that the angle at which
the Sun strikes Earth – and
the point on Earth where
it shines most directly
– changes continuously
through the year.

A year and a day

Earth is tilted at a slight angle, which means we
usually see the Sun at a slight angle, too. Yet as Earth
goes around the Sun, the angle at which we see it
changes continuously. This is why we see it rise high
in the sky on a summer's day and why it remains much
lower on a winter's day. The higher the Sun climbs
in the sky, the longer the day and
the warmer the weather. The Sun
reaches its **zenith** on midsummer's
day (the summer **solstice**), falls to
a lower and lower point every day
for six months until midwinter's
day (the winter solstice), and then
climbs higher again for six months
until the next summer solstice.

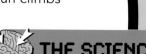

THE SCIENCE YOU LEARN:
APHELION AND PERIHELION

The Sun is not quite at the perfect centre of
Earth's orbit, so Earth moves closer to the
Sun and then further away again as it goes
round. At its closest point on 3 January, it is
147,097,800 km (91,402,300 miles) from
the Sun. This is called the perihelion. At its
furthest point, on 4 July, it is 152,098,200 km
(94,509,400 miles) away. This is the aphelion.

How long is a year?

The coming of the next summer solstice shows that Earth has completed its 939,886,398-km (584,018,332-mile) journey round the Sun. This journey takes just over 365 days, which is why the western calendar year has 365 days. The idea is that the Sun always reaches the same height in the sky on the same date each year.

Yet the match between the Sun and the calendar is never exact, because Earth actually takes 365.242 days to complete its journey, not 365 days exactly. To compensate for this, and to keep the calendar in step with Earth's movement, an extra day is added to every fourth year. This is called a leap year. One leap year is also missed out in three centuries out of four.

CUTTING EDGE: PRECISION TIMING

Even with all the adjustments made with leap years, the calendar year comes to an end about 20 seconds earlier than Earth's journey every year. So the calendar is getting more out of step with Earth each year. In fact, now scientists can measure the length of a second precisely with **atomic clocks** (see page 11), we know the problem is actually getting worse.

Each calendar day is worked out to be 86,400 seconds on the atomic clock. Yet the Earth is gradually spinning slower and slower, as the ocean tides created by the gravitational pull of the Moon (see page 24) act as a brake. The effect is that each day lasts gradually longer than the standard 86,400 seconds. Only a fraction of a second is gained each year but, over time, it all adds up. If it takes the same number of seconds to complete its orbit, it must actually take fewer days. In fact, scientists calculate that the slowing of Earth means that the calendar will be another whole day out of step by the year 7300.

Ancient cultures often aligned monuments, like this one at Stonehenge, with the winter solstice. This marked the shortest day of the year and the turning point after which the Sun begins to climb higher in the sky and the days get longer until summer arrives.

Day and night

Every 24 hours, Earth spins round completely, facing us to the Sun, then away again. This gives us day and night. Earth always spins the same way, from west to east. So, everyday, the Sun comes up (rises) in the east and goes down (sets) in the west. We are never aware of this movement, because everything else on Earth moves with us. Different places actually spin at different speeds. Places near the poles barely move at all, while places at the equator are forever speeding round at almost 40,000 km/h (25,000 mph)!

THE SCIENCE YOU LEARN: HOW IT ALL BEGAN

By measuring how old **meteorites** are, scientists have worked out that the solar system is about 4.6–5 billion years old. When it began to form, there was just a cloudy mass of stardust and gases. There were dense patches in the cloud, and the extra gravity of these dense patches began to pull dust and gases in. This clump began to spin (like water down a plug hole), creating a spinning disc. As gravity pulled it all tighter together, the dense centre became so hot that it triggered nuclear reactions, which gave birth to the Sun. Hot particles came out of the Sun (**solar wind**), blowing away all the fine dust and gas. This left just big, solid clumps, which gradually became the planets.

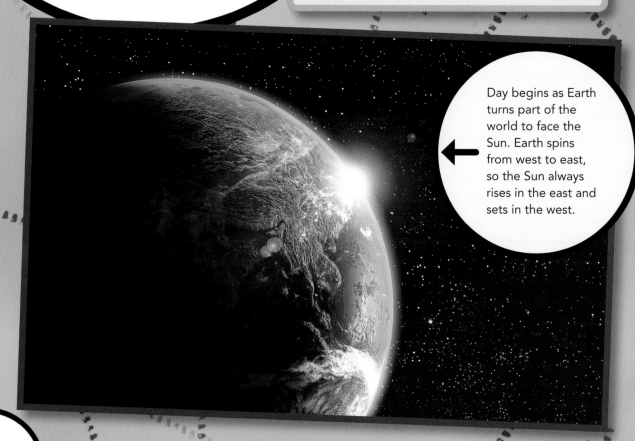

Day begins as Earth turns part of the world to face the Sun. Earth spins from west to east, so the Sun always rises in the east and sets in the west.

IN YOUR HOME:
COMPUTER TIME

The movements of the Sun and stars can give us a calendar year or a day, but for shorter times (like hours, minutes, and seconds) we need clocks. All clocks work simply by counting regular pulses. In the past, the clock's pulse was the swing of a weight on a rope, called a pendulum. Modern watches use electric vibrations inside a quartz crystal. But the most accurate pulses of all are the vibrations of energy emitted from atoms. Special machines are set up to detect these vibrations to create atomic clocks, the world's most accurate clocks. In an atomic clock, one second is defined as 9,192,631,770 vibrations of energy from a caesium-133 atom. There are only a few of these very elaborate clocks in the world. They can even send out a signal over the Internet that can be detected by a home computer! This means that your computer's clock can be set to match the accuracy of an atomic clock.

This physicist is working on a rubidium atomic clock, which is smaller and cheaper than a caesium atomic clock.

Solar days and star days

Scientists call our 24-hour day a solar day. A solar day is the time it takes Earth to spin once right round – so that the Sun is in the same position in the sky at the end of the spin as it was at the start. However, in this time, Earth spins very slightly further than once right round. This is because during the day, besides spinning, Earth rotates a little further round the Sun. So for the Sun to return to the same place in the sky, it has to spin on one degree further than a complete rotation.

The only way to measure one exact rotation of Earth is against the stars, which are so far away that they are effectively fixed in position in the night sky. By measuring how long it takes the star pattern to return to exactly the same position, you can work out the time it takes for Earth to turn once exactly. This turns out to be 23 hours, 56 minutes, and 4.09 seconds and is called a **sidereal day**.

Sun and Earth

As Earth spins on its axis and orbits around the Sun, our view of the Sun constantly changes. Of course, it is really Earth moving, but it appears as if the Sun is moving through the sky all the time.

Every day, as Earth spins, it arcs through the sky from east to west. Every day, too, this arc traces a slightly different path because Earth is moving around the Sun. The path changes because Earth is always tilted. So when Earth is on one side of the Sun, the North Pole is tilted towards it; when it is on the other side, the North Pole is tilted away. This means that the angle at which sunlight strikes Earth (known as the declination) changes all the time, as Earth moves around the Sun.

Position of Sun at midday

December path

March and September path

June path

West

North

Earth

East

As Earth journeys round the Sun, the place where it shines most directly continually shifts.

High noon

The place where the Sun reaches its highest point, or zenith, when it shines directly on Earth, gradually shifts through the year as Earth moves on. On 21 or 22 December, it reaches its zenith over the Tropic of Capricorn, south of the equator. Over the next six months, it shifts north. On the 21 or 22 June, it reaches the Tropic of Cancer, north of the equator.

The nearer places are to the zenithal Sun, the steeper the arc the Sun traces through the sky. A steep arc means the Sun is shining down most directly and intensely. The result is that places between the Tropics, where the arc is always steep, get the most powerful sunlight and so the warmest weather. Further away from the zenithal Sun, towards the poles, the Sun's arc is much shallower and the Sun is weaker, which is why polar regions are cold.

From the ground, you can see the path of the Sun through the sky changing continually through the year as Earth is at different angles.

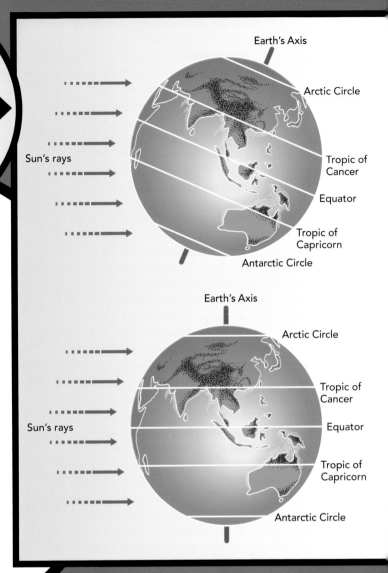

Earth's Axis

Arctic Circle

Tropic of Cancer

Equator

Tropic of Capricorn

Antarctic Circle

Sun's rays

Earth's Axis

Arctic Circle

Tropic of Cancer

Equator

Tropic of Capricorn

Antarctic Circle

Sun's rays

However, the shifting of the zenith – from north to south and back again – means the steepness of the Sun's arc varies during the year. This is what brings us seasons. We get summer when it is at its steepest, and the Sun is shining down at its most direct. We get winter when it is at its shallowest, and the Sun is raking across the landscape at a low angle, even at midday. The seasons shift from north to south with the shift of zenith. So, when there is winter in the northern hemisphere there is summer in the south, and vice versa.

THE SCIENCE YOU LEARN: SOLSTICES AND EQUINOXES

The solstices are the turning points of the year. They occur on the 21 or 22 December when the Sun is at its zenith over the southern Tropic, and 21 or 22 June when it is at its zenith over the northern Tropic. These two moments are when the Sun's path through the sky is at its steepest (summer solstice), bringing the longest day, or its shallowest (winter solstice), the shortest day. When it is the winter solstice in the southern hemisphere, it is the summer solstice in the north, and vice versa. Halfway between the solstices is the time when the zenithal sun is over the equator. This is the exact mid-point and is when day and night are the same length (12 hours each) all over the world. They occur on about 21 March and 21 September and are called the **equinoxes** (equal nights).

The shape of Earth

Pictures from space seem to show Earth as a perfectly round ball, but satellite measurements over the last 50 years have confirmed that this is not strictly true. The force of Earth's rotation flings it out at the equator so that it actually bulges out a little here, and goes flatter at the poles. So the Earth is very slightly pumpkin shaped. Scientists call this an oblate spheroid.

Earth-shaped Earth

In fact, Earth is not even a perfect oblate spheroid – it is more like a lumpy potato. Scientists usually prefer to describe Earth's shape as geoid, which just means Earth-shaped. There are obvious lumps on the Earth, such as mountains and ice caps. But there are more subtle variations, caused by differences in Earth's gravity, which mean that not even the ocean surfaces are completely smooth. Where gravity is stronger – perhaps because of a mass of dense rock beneath the surface – the sea waters are pulled in, raising the sea surface slightly.

THE SCIENCE YOU LEARN: "CENTRIFUGAL FORCE"

Anything spinning round tends to get flung out unless there is something holding it in. That is why water gets flung out of clothes in a washing machine during the spin cycle. This flinging out is so powerful that it is given the name **centrifugal force**. However, it is not really a force but an effect of momentum (see page 7). Whenever something is moving, its momentum keeps it moving in a straight line. When an object is travelling in a circle, it actually wants to travel in a straight line. The only reason it goes in a circle is because there is some force holding it on a curved path, such as gravity. The faster something is spinning, the greater its momentum, and so the greater the "centrifugal force" appears to be.

Mapping Earth

Have you ever wondered how maps of the world are made? The big problem for mapmakers (known as cartographers) is that the world is round but maps are flat. Their solution is to use **map projections**. They are called projections because the features of the round world are projected like cinema pictures on to the flat map. Imagine a light shining from inside Earth, projecting shadows of Earth's surface features on to paper. There are various kinds of projection. Each projection has its own strengths and weaknesses:

- With a planar projection, the paper is held flat. Planar projection can only show half the world at a time, but it shows true directions from one place to another.
- With a cylindrical projection, the paper is wrapped round in a roll. Cylindrical projection can show the whole world at once, but it makes countries far too wide near the poles.
- With a conical projection, the paper is curled into a cone. Conical projections are a good compromise between planar and cylindrical projection, but can show less than half the world.

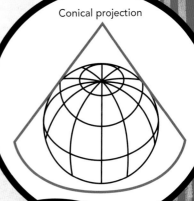

Different projections allow the features of Earth's curved surface to be mapped on flat paper.

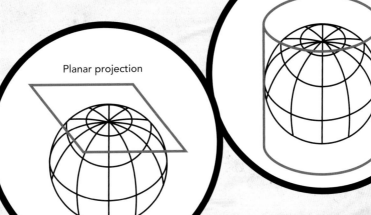

Conical projection

Cylindrical projection

Planar projection

The Moon

As it journeys through space, our tiny planet is kept constant company by the Moon. Other planets have moons but ours is very large compared to its parent planet, Earth. Although it is only about a 50th (2 percent) of Earth's volume, it is about a quarter of the diameter.

The Moon is the biggest, brightest thing in the night sky. However, it has no light of its own. It is just a big cold ball of rock, and it shines only because it reflects the light of the Sun. It is a barren, lifeless place, covered with craters created by huge lumps of rock crashing down billions of years ago when the Moon was young. The surface is completely covered in dust. There is no air, so the sky is black even during the Moon's daytime, and there is not a breath of wind to ruffle the dust.

All over the Moon are large, dark patches that people once thought were seas, which is why they are all called Mare, from the Latin for "sea". We now know, however, that they are vast, dry plains, formed by ancient lava from volcanoes that erupted early in the Moon's life.

Impact craters on the Moon, made by meteors billions of years ago, are clearly preserved because there is no water or wind to ever change their shape.

CUTTING EDGE: LUNAR BASE

In 2020, NASA plans to build a permanent base on the Moon. At first, astronauts would stay on the Moon just for a few days, but eventually, they might live there for six months or more. They would get around the Moon's surface in special cars with pressurized cabins, to save them having to wear spacesuits all the time. The first scouting mission, the Lunar Reconnaissance Orbiter, is a robot craft that will not even land. But in 2014, astronauts will finally step foot on the Moon again in the *Ares 1* spacecraft. You never know, maybe you could be one of the first people to live there!

The USA has announced plans to send more astronauts to the Moon by 2020. This computer artwork shows what a lunar base might look like. Solar panels supply power, and lunar rovers are used to travel around. A radio antenna (centre) is used to communicate with Earth.

CASE STUDY

Moon landings

The Moon is the only other world humans have ever visited. The first men to visit were the Americans Neil Armstrong and Buzz Aldrin of the *Apollo 11* space mission. They touched down on the Moon's surface on 20 July 1968. As the *Apollo* moon lander came in to land on the Moon's Sea of Tranquility, people around the world held their breath. They feared it might sink deep into the dust. Fortunately, the surface was firm enough to support the craft, and mission leader Neil Armstrong was soon able to step out on to it and say the famous words, *"That's one small step for [a] man; one giant leap for mankind"*.

Twelve men landed on the Moon between 1968 and 1972. Since then, the only Moon missions have been unmanned. This includes one by the Lunar Prospector in 1998. The Prospector found signs that there may be water (as ice) below the Moon's darkest, coldest craters. However, nothing has been confirmed.

The changing Moon

From Earth, all we can see of the Moon is the part lit up by sunlight. The part we cannot see is known as the "dark side" of the Moon. As the Moon travels round Earth, our view of it changes to reveal different amounts of each side, and so the Moon appears to change shape each night. These shape changes are called the **phases** of the Moon.

The Moon takes about a month to circle Earth, so the phases go through a monthly cycle. When the Moon is getting bigger in the first half of the month – as we see more and more of its day side – it is said to be waxing. As it gets thinner in the second half – as the day side turns away – it is said to be waning.

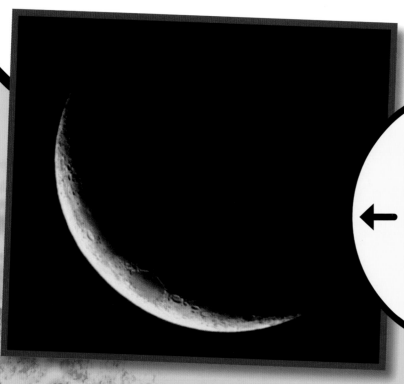

As the Moon moves between Sun and Earth, only a slim crescent of its sunlit side is visible, called the Old Moon. In the northern hemisphere the left side of the Old Moon is lit, in the southern hemisphere it is the right.

CUTTING EDGE: SPIN-ORBIT COUPLING

By what seems a strange coincidence, the Moon takes exactly the same time to spin around on its axis as it does to orbit Earth – 27.3 days. So the Moon always keeps the same side turned towards us. It now turns out that this coincidence is not a coincidence at all. The pull of Earth's gravity actually acts as a brake on the Moon's rotation, allowing it to turn only a bit at a time, like a gear wheel turning. This is called **spin-orbit coupling** or **orbital resonance**. Scientists are beginning to realize that other orbital resonances may occur in the solar system and could be what hold the rings of Saturn together.

Moon months

A month should really be called a "moonth" since that is where the word comes from. However, the Moon does not take a month to go around Earth; it only takes 27.3 days. But it takes 29.5 days to go from one full moon to the next. This is because Earth is also moving around the Sun, slightly delaying the time at which we see the full moon in the sky. This is why a "moonth", or **lunar** month, is 29.5 days. Western calendar months, however, vary from 28 days to 31 days. This is because it would be very difficult to use the Moon as a guide all the time. In 1582, Pope Gregory decided that varying the days in a month was the most practical way of fitting 12 months exactly into a year.

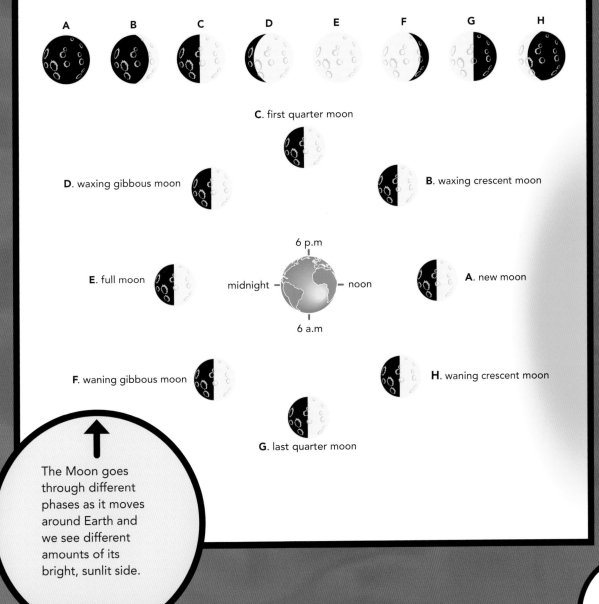

A B C D E F G H

C. first quarter moon

D. waxing gibbous moon

B. waxing crescent moon

6 p.m

midnight — noon

E. full moon

A. new moon

6 a.m

F. waning gibbous moon

H. waning crescent moon

G. last quarter moon

The Moon goes through different phases as it moves around Earth and we see different amounts of its bright, sunlit side.

Measuring Earth

The science of measuring Earth is called geodesy. Earth can be measured from the ground or from space.

INVESTIGATION: MEASURE EARTH FROM THE GROUND

There is no need to take scientists' word for the size of Earth. You can measure it if you have a friend living a few hundred kilometres away. The technique is simple, but you do need to know accurately how far away your friend lives. You can calculate Earth's size by measuring the length of the shadows cast by identical length poles at exactly the same time, around midday, on the same day. Two people will be needed in each place to make the measurements.

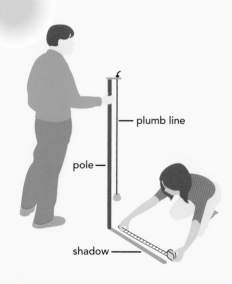

plumb line

pole

shadow

What you need:
- Three friends to help with the investigation (at least two of you need to have access to a garden or outside space)
- A calculator with tan function, or tan tables
- Two poles of identical lengths
- A tape measure
- Thread and clay for a plumb line
- A clip

1. Divide yourself and your friends into two pairs and give each pair one pole. Each pair needs to set their pole upright, outside. Use a plumb line to ensure the pole is absolutely vertical. Make a plumb line by embedding some thread inside a ball of modelling clay. Add a clip to the top of the pole and dangle the plumb line from it. Adjust the pole until the plumb line hangs completely parallel to it.
2. At exactly midday (12:00 p.m.) each pair needs to precisely measure the length of the shadow cast by the pole on the ground.
3. Next, find the angle of the Sun in each place. Do this by dividing the length of the shadow you measured in stage 2 by the length of the pole. This gives the tangent of the angle. Look in tan tables, or use the tan function of a calculator, to find out what angle this gives.
4. Subtract the angle in one place from the angle in the other. Divide the answer by 360 and multiply it by the distance between the two places (say, your garden and your friend's garden). This gives you the circumference of the world.
5. To work out the Earth's diameter, divide your circumference figure by Pi (π)— that is, 3.1415927653.

The pull of gravity is not the same all over Earth. Special satellites have revealed that there are slight variations, both from place and from time to time. The two *GRACE satellites*, for instance, travel around Earth in space about 220 km (137 miles) apart. As they fly over different parts of the world, sensitive instruments pick up any slight difference in the tug of gravity between the two that would reveal a slight local variation in gravity. From the satellite data, continually updated maps of the power of gravity around the world can be made. They detect these variations with astonishing accuracy, revealing a lot about Earth's oceans and hidden interior. The *GRACE satellites* can:

- track the movement of molten rock far below Earth's surface
- reveal the rate at which the polar ice caps are melting, by measuring minute variations of the Earth's gravitational field due to the loss of ice
- weigh just how much water has been lost in Africa in recent years, due to climate change

and human actions, such as mining and overfarming. They do this by detecting the changes in the gravity of the ground as the water is lost. Between 2003 and 2006, Africa lost 334 cubic km of water – almost as much as the whole continent actually consumed during the same time.

From 2009, the *GRACE satellites* will be complemented by the European *GOCE satellite*. Looking more like a spy plane than a satellite, it will fly as low as possible over the atmosphere. It carries three pairs of accelerometers (devices that detect the tug of gravity) so sensitive they can sense differences in gravity of 100 billionths of a percent. Such accuracy will provide much useful information about gravity variations. *GOCE*'s main mission is to track ocean currents to see how they are affected by climate change. This works because warmer currents contain less dense water, and so have a weaker gravitational pull.

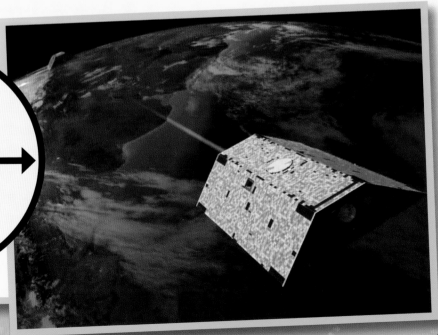

The *GRACE satellites* orbit in tandem and make linked measurements of Earth's surface using GPS (Global Positioning System) and microwave.

Eclipses

Every now and then, Earth and the Moon get between each other and the Sun. This is called an **eclipse** because the object in between eclipses (blocks out) the Sun.

A lunar eclipse is when the Moon goes behind Earth, into its shadow. This happens once or twice a year. As Earth's shadow is quite small, the Moon is only in it for a few hours. During an eclipse, the dark disc of Earth's shadow can often be seen creeping across the Moon's face. In a partial eclipse, the shadow only partly covers the Moon. In a total eclipse, the shadow completely covers it. The Moon never goes completely dark but turns a deep, rust-red colour. This happens because, although Earth blocks off direct sunlight, redder colours are deflected through Earth's atmosphere, rather like a red sky after sunset.

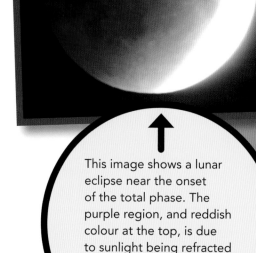

This image shows a lunar eclipse near the onset of the total phase. The purple region, and reddish colour at the top, is due to sunlight being refracted into Earth's shadow by Earth's atmosphere.

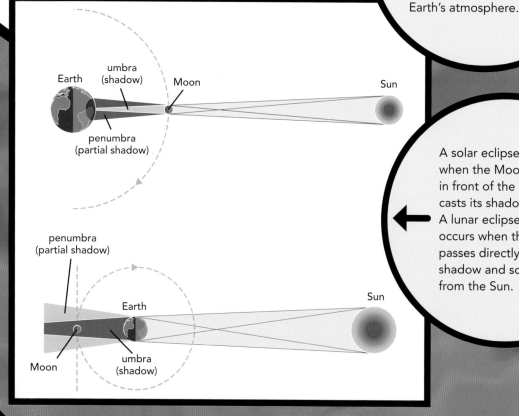

Earth

umbra (shadow)

Moon

Sun

penumbra (partial shadow)

penumbra (partial shadow)

Earth

Sun

Moon

umbra (shadow)

A solar eclipse (top) occurs when the Moon passes in front of the Sun and casts its shadow on Earth. A lunar eclipse (bottom) occurs when the Moon passes directly into Earth's shadow and so is hidden from the Sun.

Eclipse of the Sun

A solar eclipse occurs when the Moon comes between the Sun and Earth for a few minutes, casting the Moon's shadow on Earth. The Moon is quite small and far away, which means the shadow is only a few hundred kilometres wide. Only people who are in exactly the right place ever see a solar eclipse. What they see, if they look through special protective glasses, is the Moon passing in front of the Sun, darkening its disc. In a total eclipse, the Moon passes completely in front of the Sun and all that can be seen of the Sun is its **corona**. This is the only time the corona can be seen without using very special equipment. Astronomers often travel great distances to see a total eclipse.

CUTTING EDGE: LOSING ECLIPSES

Total solar eclipses are unique to Earth in the solar system because of a remarkable coincidence. Although the Moon is 400 times smaller than the Sun, it is 400 times closer to us than the Sun is. This means that the Moon appears exactly the same size as the Sun, so blocks it out exactly when it passes in front. However, measurements using laser beams, bounced off reflectors left on the Moon by Apollo mission astronauts, have recently confirmed that the Moon is gradually spinning farther and farther away from Earth, by about 4 cm (1.6 in.) a year. Scientists think this is because of the braking effect of Earth's gravity on the Moon. It means that solar eclipses are becoming less and less total, as the disc of the receding Moon gradually shrinks. Eventually, the Moon will be so small and far away that it will only ever cover a part of the Sun's face.

Total solar eclipses like this could become a thing of the past.

Tides

Twice a day, the sea rises up the shore, and then falls back again. These rises and falls, called tides, are caused by the tug of gravity between the Moon and Earth. The Moon may be far away, but the pull between them is quite enough to stretch Earth out in a slight oval. Earth is too rigid to be distorted by more than 20 cm (8 in), but because ocean waters can flow freely, the effect on the oceans is more dramatic. A bulge of water over a metre high is created on each side of the world.

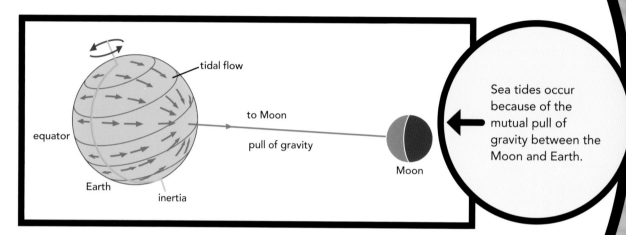

tidal flow

to Moon

equator

pull of gravity

Moon

Earth

inertia

Sea tides occur because of the mutual pull of gravity between the Moon and Earth.

As the gravitational attraction between the Moon and Earth is so strong, on the side of Earth nearest the Moon there is a bulge in the oceans towards the Moon. Gravity is stronger than momentum or inertia (see page 6). However, the gravitational force on the far side of Earth is not as strong because it is further away from the Moon. Here, momentum is stronger. This causes another bulge as the water resists gravity.

As the tidal bulge passes on around the world the sea ebbs away to low tide, exposing mud and sand. The effect is especially marked in tidal river estuaries like this.

Earth spins round, but these bulges stay in the same place, opposite the Moon. The bulges seem to run around the world, making the tide rise and fall twice a day as they pass.

Spring and neap tides

The Sun may be far away but it is so massive that it also affects the tides. When the Moon and Sun line up at the Full Moon and New Moon (see page 19), their pulling power combines to create extreme high and low tides called **spring tides**. When they are at right angles to each other, at the Half Moon, they counteract each other, creating very shallow **neap tides**.

Putting the brakes on Earth

As the tidal bulges flow round Earth, they encounter places where they run up against barriers, or move through such shallow water that there is significant friction between the water and the seabed. These obstacles make the oceans act exactly like the brakes of a car, slowing Earth down as it spins. The effect is tiny, slowing Earth enough to make the day last only one second longer every 62,500 years. But this one second is enough to make total solar eclipses occur in different places on Earth each time.

CASE STUDY

Tidal power

In the 1960s, it was thought that the huge amounts of water lifted by the tides every day might provide a renewable, clean source of energy. A huge tidal power station has been built on the mouth of the River Rance in France. This collects water (known as ponding) at high tide, then steadily lets it flow back out past turbines to generate electricity. Few more have been built, as such tidal barrages do tremendous damage to the environment, and only a few sites are suitable. Recently, however, engineers have been experimenting with tide stream generators. These are like wind power turbines deep down on the seabed, and are continuously driven by tidal currents. If they prove practical, they could provide huge amounts of clean sustainable power.

The Sun

The Sun is a star, just like all the stars in the night sky. In fact, it is a medium-sized star in the middle of its 10 billion-year life. But it is very close to us – just 150 million km (93 million miles) away, rather than billions of kilometres away like other stars. Like all stars, it is incredibly hot. Huge pressures inside the Sun boost temperatures to 15 million°C (27 million°F). This heat turns the surface into a raging inferno that glows so brightly that it lights Earth, giving us daylight.

The chromosphere (orange) lies above the Sun's photosphere. It mainly consists of hydrogen gas.

The anatomy of the Sun

The Sun is made mainly of two gases: hydrogen and helium. Using a technique called helioseismology, scientists have probed below the Sun's surface. Telescopes orbiting Earth in space constantly monitor the Sun to detect subtle pulsations on the Sun's surface. Just like earthquake waves reveal the nature of Earth's interior, so these pulsations have shown that the Sun, too, has a layered interior. They show that, like Earth, it has a core, where most of the heat is generated. The heat takes 10 million years to rise to the surface, passing through several layers, including the **photosphere**, a forest of flames (called the **chromosphere**), and the corona. Temperatures in the photosphere reach 5,000°C (9,032°F), enough to melt almost any substance. An astronaut coming within half a million kilometres would be instantly roasted alive by the heat – or killed by the deadly radiation it emits.

The minimal distance between the Sun and us is very valuable for astronomers. It makes the Sun the only star close enough to reveal its surface and show that stars have atmospheres. The Sun has been crucial in allowing astronomers to see how the size and mass of a star relates to its brightness. Close study of the colours of light emitted by the Sun also reveal what it is made of. It has enabled scientists to build up a very detailed picture of what stars are and how they evolve. In this way, we can work out a great deal about other stars, galaxies, and even the universe itself.

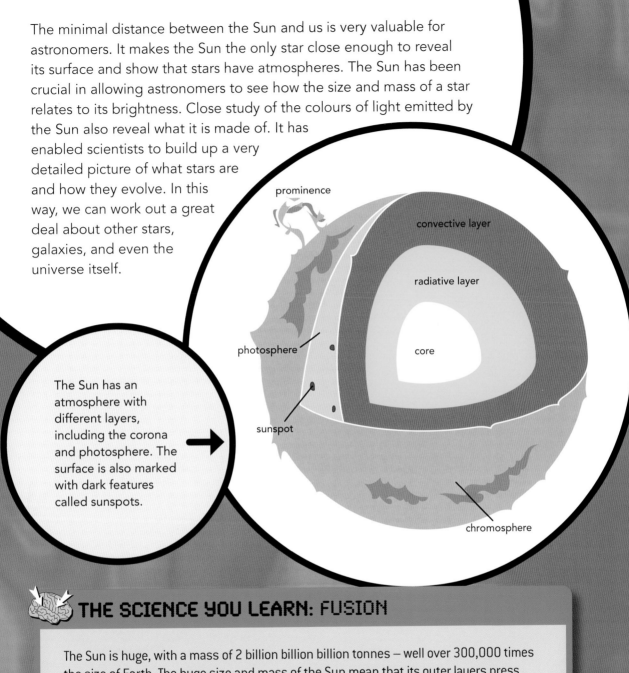

prominence

convective layer

radiative layer

photosphere

core

sunspot

chromosphere

The Sun has an atmosphere with different layers, including the corona and photosphere. The surface is also marked with dark features called sunspots.

THE SCIENCE YOU LEARN: FUSION

The Sun is huge, with a mass of 2 billion billion billion tonnes – well over 300,000 times the size of Earth. The huge size and mass of the Sun mean that its outer layers press in with huge pressure. This squeezes the hydrogen gases in the Sun's centre, heating it up and turning it into a nuclear bomb. The pressure in the Sun's core is so gigantic that hydrogen atoms are forced (fused) together to make helium atoms, in a process called **nuclear fusion**. As they fuse, the atoms release huge amounts of energy. This is what happens inside a hydrogen bomb but, in the Sun, it is on a very different scale. The energy created in the Sun's core is the equivalent of 100 billion hydrogen bombs exploding every second!

Solar power

The Sun's photosphere glows with amazing brightness. Each 6 cm²
(1 in²) of the Sun's surface burns with the brightness of 1.5 million
candles. The photosphere is so brilliant that it floodlights the entire
solar system, beaming out heat and light at 300,000 km (186,000 miles)
per second in all directions.

Sunlight reaches the Earth in just eight minutes, filling the atmosphere
with heat, energy, and light. Only a minute fraction of the Sun's output
hits Earth, but this is more than enough to provide our planet with nearly
all its energy. Without it, Earth would be darker than the darkest night
and much colder than the Antarctic.

THE SCIENCE YOU LEARN: RADIATION AND THE SPECTRUM

Light from a torch, microwaves for cooking, and cosmic rays from the Sun are all kinds of radiation.
Radiation is basically energy on the move, and an atom's way of getting rid of excess energy.
Sometimes, radiation is in the form of high-energy particles, pushed out by the nuclei of unstable
atoms as they break up. At other times, radiation is tiny waves, such as light and radio waves,
emitted by the atom's electrons. These waves, called electromagnetic waves, are almost pure
energy, and they come in a broad spectrum (range) of different wavelengths.

Radiation from the Sun contains the entire electromagnetic spectrum.
A small portion (just over 40 percent) of it is visible light – the light
we see – and is positioned in the middle of the spectrum. About
50 percent of the Sun's radiation is long-wave radiation and is
positioned at one end of the spectrum. These waves are too
long for our eyes to see, such as microwaves. At the other end
of the spectrum is short-wave radiation (which accounts for
just less than 10 percent). These waves are too short for our
eyes to see and include X-rays.

Electromagnetic
radiation comes in a
whole range (spectrum)
of different wavelengths.

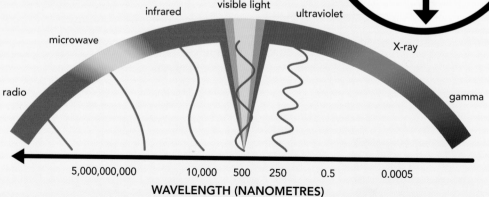

The Sun and Earth

As the Sun's rays hit Earth, 20 percent is trapped in the atmosphere, and 30 percent is reflected straight back into space. Less than half gets through to the ground. The atmosphere lets through short-wave radiation very easily, but not long-wave radiation. These waves pass through the atmosphere to warm the ground, but don't warm the atmosphere very much. Instead, the lower layers of the atmosphere are warmed by the reflection and re-radiation of the Sun's rays from the ground, in the form of long-wave radiation.

This is why there is a so-called greenhouse effect. Like panes of glass in a greenhouse, certain gases in the atmosphere (greenhouse gases) let through short-wave radiation from the Sun, but block long-wave radiation, such as infrared rays reflected back from the ground. The result is that heat gets trapped on Earth's surface. Greenhouse gases include carbon dioxide and methane. These gases occur naturally, but they have increased dramatically in recent years due to human activity. Most scientists agree that this increase is responsible for the warming of Earth's climate.

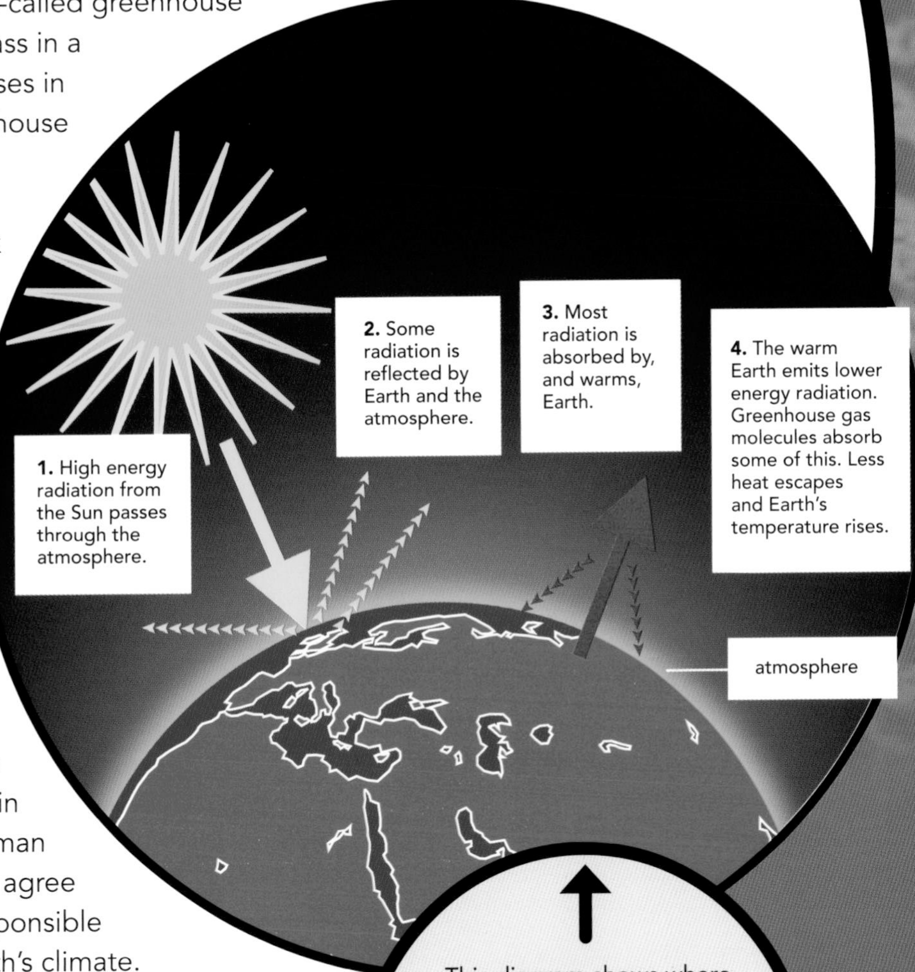

1. High energy radiation from the Sun passes through the atmosphere.

2. Some radiation is reflected by Earth and the atmosphere.

3. Most radiation is absorbed by, and warms, Earth.

4. The warm Earth emits lower energy radiation. Greenhouse gas molecules absorb some of this. Less heat escapes and Earth's temperature rises.

atmosphere

This diagram shows where the energy goes when sunlight hits Earth. Barely half reaches the ground, and almost two-thirds of that is re-radiated back into space.

Most of Earth is protected by its magnetic fields from the high energy particles that stream from the Sun in the solar wind. But they leak into Earth's atmosphere above the poles, creating the spectacular Aurorae light shows, seen here from space, as they collide with gas particles in the air.

Solar variation

Studying the Sun can be a dangerous activity, and many astronomers have been blinded by looking at it for too long. With special equipment, however, astronomers have been able to discover that the Sun's surface is continually changing. High magnification telescopes, with dark viewing filters, reveal that the surface is dotted with thousands of gas cells, called granules, which bubble up for anything from a few minutes to half an hour. Larger, slightly hotter patches (called faculae) appear every now and then. As do occasionally bright loops of flame (called prominences) that roll out from the Sun's surface.

More spectacular, however, are **solar flares**. These are brilliant explosions of energy and radiation that shoot out glowing gusts of particles far above the Sun's surface. Solar flares can create high-speed gusts in the solar wind, called solar storms. These can rip into Earth's atmosphere, creating spectacular light shows in the polar skies, called aurorae. They also cause power surges in electricity supply systems, which can cause black-outs.

Sunspots

With special viewing equipment, it is possible to see that there are dark spots on the Sun's surface. They are called sunspots and are patches in the photosphere where the temperature is about 2,000°C (3,600°F) cooler. They occur where the Sun's magnetic field has broken through the photosphere and blocked off energy rising from the Sun's interior. They usually appear in groups, and seem to drift across the face of the Sun over the course of two weeks. They only appear to move, however, because the Sun spins on its axis, taking about just under a month to spin right round. Sunspots are short-lived, and rarely make the journey across the face of the Sun more than once or twice.

The number of sunspots varies, reaching a maximum every 11 years, when some sunspots can be up to 100,000 km (60,000 miles) across – many times the size of Earth. Scientists speculate about the possibility that the weather on Earth is slightly cooler at the time of sunspot maximums. The last maximum was in 2000, so we can expect another in 2011 or 2012. However, there was a period between 1645 and 1715, called the Maunder minimum, in which sunspots virtually disappeared. The world's weather in some places turned so cold that the period is now called the Little Ice Age.

Some scientists believe that a rise in the number of sunspots can affect the weather on Earth.

Solar wind

As the Sun's corona heats up, it pumps out a million tonnes of electrically charged and radioactive particles every second. These particles stream out in every direction in what is called the solar wind. They travel at speeds of more than 400 km (250 miles) per second. The particles take about four days to stream across space and blast past Earth. Fortunately, we are shielded from this deadly wind by Earth's magnetic field, which extends far out into space. Deflected by the field, most of the particles wash around Earth harmlessly.

The planets

The rocky planets

The four planets nearest to the Sun are, in order: Mercury, Venus, Earth, and Mars. All four are small compared to most of the planets further out, such as Jupiter. These four planets are sometimes called the terrestrial, or Earth-like, planets. Unlike the giant outer planets, they are made mostly of rock, and have hard surfaces on which a spacecraft could land. In fact, space probes have landed on both Venus and Mars, the nearest planets to Earth. All the rocky planets have an atmosphere of gas – although Mercury's is almost nonexistent – but they are very different.

Mercury is the nearest planet of all to the Sun, often less than 58 million km (36 million miles) away. With almost no atmosphere to protect it, temperatures on the side facing the Sun soar to 425°C (800°F) while the dark side plummets to −180°C (−290°F). Mercury is so close to the Sun it travels round it in just 88 days (compared to 365 days for Earth). Yet it spins very slowly, taking over 58 Earth days. So there are less than two days in Mercury's year.

The channels on this crater wall are thought to show the presence of liquid water in Mars' recent history. It is thought that these features are not very old, which means that liquid water may exist below the surface of Mars.

Venus is almost exactly the same size as Earth. It is about 12,000 km (7,500 miles) across, and weighs about 20 percent less than Earth. However, Venus is quite unlike Earth. Its atmosphere is thick with poisonous carbon dioxide and clouds of sulfuric acid. This thick atmosphere traps the Sun's heat and makes the surface a scorching desert, where temperatures rise to 470°C (875°F).

Mars is the only planet with daytime temperatures anywhere near similar to Earth's (but still much colder, see page 48) and it has an equally clear atmosphere. It is also the only other planet with much water on its surface, but the water on Mars is all frozen in ice caps (although there is evidence of liquid standing water in the past). Most of the planet is a desert, with no oceans or any sign of life – just the iron-rich, red rocks and dust that earn it the nickname "red planet". Scientists hope that space probes will eventually find traces of microscopic life under the surface.

CUTTING EDGE: MERCURY MISSION

In January 2008, the *Mercury Messenger* spacecraft flew within just 200 km (124 miles) of Mercury – the first spacecraft to go that close in 30 years. *Messenger* is now slowing down and adjusting its course so that by 2011 it can begin to orbit the planet at low level. When it does, it can begin to map the planet's surface in detail, and maybe answer a big mystery about its centre (core). Scientists believe that Mercury must have a molten metal core that churns like a dynamo to give the planet a magnetic field like Earth's.

The *Mercury Messenger* space probe is flying closer to the planet Mercury than any recent probe. As it skims above the planet's surface, it will map it in great detail.

Gas giants

Beyond Mars are four planets bigger than any of the others in the solar system: Jupiter, Saturn, Uranus, and Neptune. Jupiter and Saturn are especially huge. Jupiter is twice as heavy as all the other planets combined, and its volume is 1,300 times bigger than Earth's! Saturn is almost as big. Only a tiny core in the centre of these giant planets is rock: the rest is mainly gas. However, the gas is squeezed by the huge pressure of gravity until it is often liquid or even solid.

Jupiter

Jupiter is by far the biggest planet in the solar system – over 140,000 km (88,000 miles) across – and it takes almost 12 years to go round the Sun. Yet despite its immense bulk, it spins round faster than any other planet. In fact, it turns right round in under 10 hours, which means the surface is speeding along at almost 14,000 km/h (9,000 mph). Its surface is covered in colourful clouds of ammonia gas, whipped into storm belts by violent winds. One storm, called the Great Red Spot, is 40,000 km (25,000 miles) across and has lasted at least 300 years.

Saturn

Saturn is the second largest planet and is a pale, butterscotch-coloured ball of gas over 120,000 km (74,000 miles) across. It is known as the ringed planet because it has an amazing halo of rings circling its middle. The rings are made up of tiny chunks of ice and rock. Although the rings are barely thicker than a house, they stretch out over 80,000 km (50,000 miles) into space.

This false colour image of Saturn was taken from *Voyager 2*. Saturn is a giant gas planet.

Uranus

Uranus is so far from the Sun that its surface is unimaginably cold. Temperatures in the outer layers of Uranus drop to –210°C (–346°F)! In this bitter cold, even the gas methane forms clouds of ice, giving the planet its striking blue colour. Below the clouds are deep oceans of liquid water and ammonia.

Neptune

Neptune is the fourth largest planet in the solar system. Like Uranus, Neptune is covered in clouds of methane crystals, which give it a beautiful cobalt blue colour. It is so far from the Sun – about 4.5 billion km (2.8 billion miles) away – that it takes 164.79 years to spin round. It hasn't even completely circled the Sun once since it was first discovered in 1846!

CUTTING EDGE: EUROPA'S OCEAN

Jupiter was the first planet seen to have moons. They were discovered in 1610 by Galileo; the four moons are now called Galilean moons. Astronomers are discovering new moons for Jupiter all the time, using ultra-powerful telescopes. They now know of 63, but there could be more. It is Europa, one of the Galilean moons, however, that is fascinating scientists the most. Europa is entirely covered by ice. However, studying subtly detectable magnetic and gravity effects on neighbouring moons, and radar scans taken from passing space probes, scientists have detected a liquid ocean under the ice. The ocean liquid is water and may just contain the best possibility of life in the solar system outside Earth.

Titan is Saturn's largest moon. The spacecraft *Cassini* took this image in 2006. Infrared and radar sensors were used to take pictures because Titan has a thick atmosphere of nitrogen, which makes it difficult to see surface features.

Space debris

As well as eight large planets, the solar system contains countless smaller objects. All the planets except Venus and Mercury have moons or satellites circling them. Beyond Neptune lies the small ball of rock called Pluto (which was once classified as the ninth planet) along with its companion, Charon. Then there are hundreds of thousands of lumps of rock, metal, and ice, called asteroids. Most circle the Sun in the asteroid belt, between Mars and Jupiter, and may be debris from the early days of the solar system that never properly formed a planet. Satellites and asteroids generally move steadily around the Sun or their planet. Yet other objects, such as comets and **meteoroids**, hurtle round in various directions – and can crash into planets.

Meteoroids

Meteoroids are chunks of rock and iron that have come away from asteroids and comets. Many meteoroids collide with Earth, but are usually so tiny they burn up as they crash into Earth's atmosphere. As they burn up they leave bright, glowing trails in the night sky, earning them the name **meteors** or shooting stars. Occasionally, Earth collides with a big clump of meteoroids, creating a shower of shooting stars. Meteoroids are sometimes large enough to make it through the atmosphere. Most of these objects, called **meteorites**, are smaller than a tennis ball, but a few are much bigger.

Meteors, streaking past stars, light the night sky over a bedouin tent near Amman, Jordan in the Middle East, in the early hours of August 12, 2004. The Perseid meteor shower is sparked every August when Earth passes through a stream of space debris left by Comet Swift-Tuttle.

Comets

Comets are lumps of ice filled with dust and rock. Each one travels round the Sun in a giant orbit that – more often than not – is in the outer reaches of the solar system. But when comets swing in close to the Sun, they partly melt, and then throw out a vast tail of dust and gas that glistens in the Sun. This makes for a brief but spectacular show in the night sky.

About 50,000 years ago a huge meteorite struck Arizona, USA. It weighed about 300,000 tonnes, was about 50 m (164 ft) in diameter, and was travelling at a speed of 12.8 km/second (28,600 mph). The impact left a crater nearly 1.5 km (0.9 miles) wide and about 170 m (558 ft) deep.

CUTTING EDGE: DWARF PLANETS

For a long time, there were thought to be nine planets in the solar system with Pluto the smallest and most remote. But in recent years dozens of small rocky objects, much the same size as Pluto, have been spotted beyond Neptune, in what is called the Kuiper Belt. This includes one dubbed Xena (now known as Eris) and another called Sedna, both of which are much the same size as Pluto. Astronomers wondered for a while whether to regard Eris or Sedna as the tenth planet. But what about all the other objects: should they be called planets, too? In August 2006, astronomers met and decided that the best solution was to demote Pluto from planet status. From now on, Pluto and all these other objects are to be called plutoids.

Space travel

The age of space travel dawned less than 50 years ago, when the tiny Russian satellite *Sputnik 1* was blasted into space in 1957. Since then hundreds of spacecraft have travelled through the solar system and even beyond. In 1969, the astronauts of *Apollo 11* set foot on the Moon. In 1976, the *Viking 1* robot space probe landed on Mars. In 1973, *Pioneer 10* reached Jupiter. Now *Voyager 2* has almost flown out of the solar system.

Slowly the boundaries of exploration are being pushed back, as robot spacecraft investigate the nearby planets in detail. Meanwhile, a rising number of satellites are circling Earth itself, telling us more about our planet and bringing a revolution in telecommunications.

CUTTING EDGE: SPACE TRIPPERS

At the moment only government astronauts and a few extremely wealthy individuals get to travel in a spacecraft. But some companies are now developing spacecraft that could get up near space so cheaply and easily that people who were only moderately rich could go up in them for suborbital day trips (suborbital means almost but not quite in space). In 2004, a private spacecraft called *SpaceShipOne* that flies like a plane made successful test flights 112 km (69 miles) up. In 2007, another spacecraft called *Blue Origin* made a successful test flight. Virgin Galactic plans to build five *SpaceShipTwo* craft to carry paying passengers up into space by the end of 2009.

NASA's *Galileo* spacecraft took this picture of Jupiter's moon, Io.

Getting lift off

To escape from the pull of Earth's gravity and launch a spacecraft into space demands enormous power. Travelling through the emptiness of space doesn't, however. So spacecraft are usually boosted into space by powerful launch vehicles, which are rockets designed to fall away in stages when the spacecraft is on its way. These disposable stages are little more than giant fuel tanks with rocket burners on the bottom, some burning liquid oxygen and hydrogen, and some burning solid fuel. The biggest launch vehicle of all was the Russian Energia rocket, which could deliver a thrust of over 3 million kilograms.

For over 30 years, the Space Shuttle craft have been the main way for astronauts to orbit above Earth, but it is now coming to the end of its operational life.

Robot spacecraft

In the early days, manned spacecraft could only be used once, with just a tiny capsule holding astronauts as they fell back to Earth. Now, astronauts are carried up into orbit above Earth by shuttlecraft, which can take off and land again and again, like an aeroplane. The Russian version was known as the *Buran* ("snowstorm"), the American version is known as the Space Shuttle.

Humans have only been to the Moon, but robot spacecraft have now visited all the planets in the solar system. Among the most successful probes was the *Galileo* mission, which reached Jupiter in 1995, and sent back some stunning pictures of the planet's surface. It then went on to explore Jupiter's moons, before plunging to its doom on Jupiter in September 2003.

Artificial satellites

Since *Sputnik 1*, the first artificial satellite launched in 1957, many thousands more have been launched into space. In fact, so many have been launched and reached the end of their useful life that the band of space in which satellites orbit is now littered with pieces of space junk. This can range from tiny scraps no bigger than a screw to entire rockets!

Satellites have many different purposes. Some are space telescopes, such as the Hubble, designed to look into space from beyond Earth's cloudy atmosphere. Some are communications satellites that beam anything from television pictures to telephone messages around the world. Some are navigation satellites, like the Global Positioning System (GPS), that enable people to locate their position very accurately using signals from a network of satellites.

The European Remote-Sensing Satellite 2 was launched in April 1995. It contained instruments to measure sea surface temperatures and wind speed and direction. It orbits around 785 km (488 miles) above Earth.

Observation satellites

Perhaps the most interesting scientifically, however, are the observation satellites. These are designed to look down on Earth. Some are spy satellites, like the *Ikon/Keyhole* satellites. These have such high resolution that they can read the cover of a book on Earth from high up in space! But there are many others that have enabled scientists to study Earth in an entirely new way.

- The *TOPEX/Poseidon* satellite can measure variations in the height of the ocean surface of just a few centimetres. This amazing accuracy has revealed hidden mountains on the seabed. The extra pull of gravity above the mountains, deep in the ocean, created tiny differences in the height of the sea surface. Scientists could create a complete map of the unknown ocean depths.
- NASA's *Aqua* satellite can detect soil moisture. This is useful for farmers to tell if crops need watering or when the soil is ready for planting.
- Satellite images can be used to: assess crop yields; search for minerals and petroleum deposits; identify earthquake-prone areas; chart the meanderings of the Gulf Stream, and other currents that affect our weather and climate; search for shipwrecks on the seabed.
- Satellite pictures help us gauge how human activities are affecting the planet. They document the destruction of rainforests, monitor water temperatures in the ocean, and measure the warming of Earth's atmosphere.
- Satellites can reveal whether a crop plant has just been planted or is ready for harvest, if it is suffering from a disease or being attacked by pests.
- Satellites reveal geology and land forms where oil or minerals may lay, or even traces of minerals on the surface. Each mineral also has its own spectral signature. Satellites have revealed deposits of: copper, nickel, zinc, and uranium in the United States; tin in Brazil; and copper in Mexico.
- Weather satellites record cloud patterns and movements that help predict storms. They also measure temperature, moisture in the atmosphere, air pressure, rainfall, and snow depth.
- Satellites can track large fires, wildlife outfitted with radio transmitters, glaciers calving into icebergs, and changes in the size of the hole in the ozone layer.

Amazing journeys

Except for the manned missions to the Moon, all the space probes sent off to explore the solar system have been robot craft. Some of these have travelled astonishing distances. In September 2008, *Voyager 1* and *2* were on the edge of the solar system, about to pass into the blackness of deep space, after journeys of 16 billion and 13 billion km.

Probe landings

Robot probes have told us a huge amount about the solar system. Most of them are fly-bys, which means they spend just a few days or weeks passing their target, making observations, and beaming back data, before passing on. Landings are rare, but when they do occur, like the Mars Pathfinder landings on Mars in 1997, they are tremendously exciting for those watching their progress back on Earth. This is why another Mars lander will soon be on its way to Mars, carrying the Mars Science Laboratory rover, which will help analyze the planet and look for signs of microbial life.

In this image, released in 2004, NASA's Mars Exploration Rover *Opportunity* is examining rock on the El Capitan area of the planet using tools on its robotic arm.

Probing asteroids and comets

With fantastic pictures now taken by robot probes of all the planets except Mercury, probes are now being sent out to explore the asteroids and comets, and the farthest reaches of the solar system. In 2007, NASA launched the *Dawn* probe to investigate the largest asteroids, Ceres and Vesta, while the Japanese *Hayabusa* mission set off to attempt a soft landing on the asteroid Itokawa. The European Space Agency's Rosetta mission is on its way to meet with the Comet Churyumov-Gerasimenko in 2014, then accompany it as it moves in towards the Sun. NASA's *New Horizons* probe is headed far out to Pluto in 2015 and then on to other dwarf planets in the Kuiper Belt.

CUTTING EDGE:
POWERING UNMANNED MISSIONS

One of the problems with long space voyages is providing the fuel to keep the unmanned spacecraft going on such a long journey. Scientists have been trying to develop new kinds of propulsion systems. More and more unmanned missions are now using ion drives that were first developed for NASA's Deep Space probes in the late 1990s. The ion engine, first built in 1960, works by first removing electrons from a gas called xenon. This turns the xenon atoms into electrically charged atoms called ions. The ionized gas is then squeezed out between two grids, with the opposite electrical charge of the ions, at speeds of 100,000 km/h (60,000 mph). The craft is driven along by this stream of ions.

Satellites need to stay up in space for years, but sometimes they need to make adjustments to their position, which means they need motors that can be started up easily without any fuel. Scientists are now working on solar-powered engines. These use the warmth of the Sun to heat a liquid, such as water or ammonia, to very high temperatures. The hot liquid is then shot out in a jet to propel the satellite on its new course.

Human missions

Since Russian cosmonaut Yuri Gagarin made the first human spaceflight in 1961, hundreds of astronauts have travelled into space. Six missions took astronauts to the Moon (see page 17) but most simply take them up a little way above Earth.

Living in space

Some of these short missions are for maintaining or adjusting satellites, but in recent years many have been trips to space stations. Space stations are craft that hang in space, as they continually orbit Earth. They provide a home in space for astronauts and scientists and, more recently, the occasional high-paying tourist. They are built up in space bit by bit in a series of missions. The current space station, the International Space Station, is the biggest yet – 110 m (361 ft) long, and provides as much living space as a five-bedroomed house!

This astronaut performs a space walk during the construction of the International Space Station in 2002.

After men landed on the Moon, people imagined it would not be long before astronauts would be heading off for other planets. However, that is now looking very unlikely. The problem is that the distances (even to the nearest planet, Mars) are far too great for astronauts to endure the journey. Moreover, no one has yet found a way of building a spacecraft that could land on Mars, then take off, and make a return trip. Scientists are hoping that humans might one day go back to the Moon. Even that is likely to be up to a decade away.

This artist's impression shows what a manned space mission to Mars could look like.

THE SCIENCE YOU LEARN: WEIGHTLESSNESS

Unless astronauts orbiting Earth in space stations and spacecraft wear boots that lock into the ground, they float around as if entirely weightless. Astronauts spend considerable time training underwater to get used to this weightlessness. Weightlessness can create quite a few problems for everyday living. The toilet, for instance, has to have suction devices to get rid of waste. People sometimes assume that astronauts are weightless in space because they are beyond the influence of Earth's gravity. This is not true; they are not actually weightless at all.

What is really happening is that the spacecraft hurtles round Earth so fast that it counteracts the effect of gravity. It is as if the astronauts are in an elevator falling so fast that they float off the floor. Fortunately, the astronauts' elevator never reaches the ground!

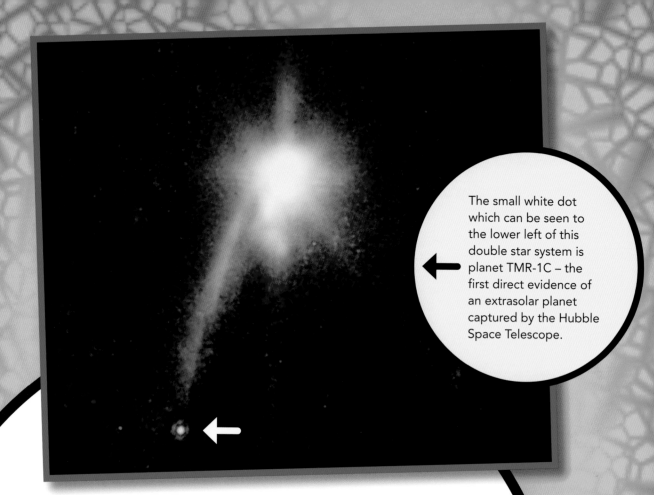

The small white dot which can be seen to the lower left of this double star system is planet TMR-1C – the first direct evidence of an extrasolar planet captured by the Hubble Space Telescope.

Beyond the solar system

Over the last 50 years, scientists have discovered a huge amount of our solar system both by looking through telescopes and from space probes. However, relatively recently they made an astonishing new discovery: our solar system is not the only one! They had guessed that this might be so but, in October 1995, Didier Queloz and Michel Mayor – of the Geneva Observatory in Switzerland – confirmed it. They announced they had discovered a planet circling another sun-like star far away, called 51 Pegasi.

Since then, astronomers have discovered over 300 more planets circling distant stars, like the planets of our solar system circle the Sun. These planets are called **extrasolar planets**, or exoplanets, because they are outside the solar system. They are much too far away to see directly, but they can be detected in various ways. One way they reveal themselves is by the way their gravity makes their star wobble slightly. Another is by the way a planet bends the light from the star.

THE SCIENCE YOU LEARN: LIGHT YEARS

Beyond the solar system, distances are so huge that it makes no sense to measure them in kilometres or miles. Even the nearest star, Proxima Centauri, is over 40 trillion km away. The furthest star cluster is over 100 billion trillion km away (that's 100 followed by 21 zeros)! So astronomers measure the distance to the stars in light-years instead. A light-year is the distance that light, the fastest thing in the universe, travels in a year. Light travels 299,792 km (186,282 miles) in a second. In a year, it travels 9,459,724,032,000 km (5,878,000,000,000 miles). This means that one light-year measures nearly 10 trillion km (6 trillion miles).

"Super-Earths"

Most of the extrasolar planets discovered so far are giants, at least as big as Jupiter, and made of gas. Such big planets are easier to see. What scientists really wanted to see are smaller, rocky planets, not that much bigger than Earth, which might be suitable for life.

In early 2005, a team led by Geoff Marcy at the University of California, USA, found one! It was named Gliese 876d. Gliese 876d is circling far too close to its star to be able to support life. It is incredibly hot. Soon after Marcy's discovery, scientists were finding more and more "super-Earths" (so-called because they are made of rock like Earth, but are much bigger).

In January 2006, astronomers spotted a super-Earth, a little bigger than Earth, circling a red dwarf star 22,000 light-years away. It was probably too far away from its star and so too cold for life. Since 70 percent of the stars in our Milky Way galaxy are red dwarfs, the discovery hinted that there could be many, many more of these Earth-size planets. The search is now on for a "Goldilocks" super-Earth planet, which – like Earth – is neither too hot nor too cold for life. In May 2008, astronomers at the HARPS observatory in Chile announced that they had spotted no less than 45 small new planets, many of which could be super-Earths! Could one of these be like Earth?

Facts and figures

Planets

Mercury

Distance from the Sun: minimum 45.9 million km (28.5 million miles); maximum 69.7 million km (43.2 million miles).
Diameter at the equator: 4,878 km (3,024 miles).
Time taken to orbit the Sun: 88 Earth days.
Day (single rotation): 58.6 Earth days.
Tilt: 2°.
Mass: 0.055 of Earth.
Surface temperature: –180 to 430°C (–292 to 806°F).
Number of moons: 0.

Venus

Distance from the Sun: minimum 107.4 million km (66.6 million miles); maximum 109 million km (67.58 million miles).
Diameter at the equator: 12,102 km (7,503 miles).
Time taken to orbit the Sun: 224.7 Earth days.
Day (single rotation): 243.01 Earth days.
Tilt: 177.3°.
Mass: 0.82 of Earth.
Surface temperature: 470°C (878°F).
Number of moons: 0.

Earth

Distance from the Sun: minimum 146 million km (90.5 million miles); maximum 152 million km (94 million miles).
Diameter at the equator: 12,756.2 km (7,908.8 miles).
Time taken to orbit the Sun: 365.26 Earth days.

Day (single rotation): 24 hours.
Tilt: 23.44°.
Surface temperature: –89 to 57.7°C (–128.2 to 135.86°F).
Number of moons: 1.

Mars

Distance from the Sun: minimum 206.7 million km (128 million miles); maximum 249 million km (154 million miles).
Diameter at the equator: 6,786 km (4,207 miles).
Time taken to orbit the Sun: 687 Earth days.
Day (single rotation): 24.62 hours.
Tilt: 25.19°.
Mass: 0.11 of Earth.
Surface temperature: –87 to –5°C (–124.6 to 23°F).
Number of moons: 2 (Phobos and Deimos).

Jupiter

Distance from the Sun: minimum 740.9 million km (459 million miles); maximum 815.7 million km (505.7 million miles).
Diameter at the equator: 142,984 km (8,865 miles).
Time taken to orbit the Sun: 11.86 Earth years.
Day (single rotation): 9.84 hours.
Tilt: 3.1°.
Mass: 318 Earths.
Surface temperature: –150°C (–238°F).
Number of moons: 63 so far discovered, including the four big Galilean moons (Europa, Callisto, Ganymede, and Io), plus

many smaller ones (including Metis, Adrastea, Amalthea, and Thebe). Moons, like Leda, Himalia, Lysithea, and Elara, are captured meteorites. The Ananke, Carme, Pasiphaë, and Sinope moons orbit backwards.

Saturn

Distance from the Sun: minimum 1,347 million km (835 million miles); maximum 1,507 million km (934 million miles).
Diameter at the equator 120,536 km (74,732 miles).
Time taken to orbit the Sun: 29.46 Earth years.
Day (single rotation): 10.23 hours.
Tilt: 26.7°.
Mass: 95.18 Earths.
Surface temperature: –180°C (–292°F).
Number of Moons: 60 so far discovered, including Titan (the biggest known moon), Iapetus, Enceladus, Rhea, Dione, and Mimas. The moon Phoebe orbits in reverse.

Uranus

Distance from the Sun: minimum 2,735 million km (1,695 million miles); maximum 3,004 million km (1,862 million miles).
Diameter at the equator: 51,118 km (31,693 miles).
Time taken to orbit the Sun: 84.01 Earth years.
Day (single rotation): 17.9 hours.
Tilt: 98°.
Mass: 14.53 Earths.
Surface temperature: –210°C (–346°F).

Number of moons: 27 so far discovered. All except Umbriel are named mainly after characters in Shakespeare's plays, including Cordelia, Miranda, Juliet, Desdemona, and Titania.

Neptune

Distance from the Sun: minimum 4,456 million km (2,762 million miles); maximum 4,537 million km (2,813 million miles).
Diameter at the equator: 49,528 km (30,707 miles).
Time taken to orbit the Sun: 164.79 Earth years.
Day (single rotation): 16 hours.
Tilt: 29.6°.
Mass: 17.14 Earths.
Surface temperature: –210°C (–346°F).
Number of moons: 13 so far discovered. All are named after characters in Greek myths, especially those linked to the sea god Poseidon. They include Triton, Proteus, Thalassa, Galatea, Naiad, Despina, Larissa, and Nereid. Neptune's biggest moon, Triton, has the coldest temperature yet recorded in the solar system at –236°C (–392.8°F).

Dwarf planets and other plutoids

Five of these dwarf planets have so far been recognized: Ceres, Pluto, Eris, Makemake, and Haumea. Ceres is also an asteroid and is the only one nearer than Neptune. The other four are also called "plutoids", which is the term for any planetlike object out beyond Neptune. Besides these four, astronomers know of six other plutoids that are more than 1,000 km (620 miles) across: Sedna, Quaoar, Orcus, Ixion, Varuna, and 2002 AW197.

Ceres

Distance from the Sun: minimum 381 million km (236 million miles); maximum 447 million km (277 million miles).
Diameter at the equator: 974 km (603 miles).
Time taken to orbit the Sun: 4.6 Earth years.
Day (single rotation): 6.39 Earth days.
Tilt: 3°.
Mass: 0.00012 Earths.
Surface temperature: −206 to −134°C (−338.8 to −209.2°F).
Number of moons: 0.

Eris (formerly Xena)

Distance from the Sun: minimum 5.3 billion km (3.3 billion miles); maximum 14.6 billion km (9 billion miles).
Diameter at the equator: 2,400 km (1,488 miles).
Time taken to orbit the Sun: 558 Earth years.
Tilt: 44°.
Surface temperature: −243°C (−405.4°F).
Number of moons: 1.

Haumea

Distance from the Sun: minimum 5.2 billion km (3.2 billion miles); maximum 7.6 billion km (4.7 billion miles).
Diameter at the equator: 1,400 km (868 miles).
Time taken to orbit the Sun: 285.4 Earth years.
Day (single rotation): approximately 4 hours.
Tilt: 28°.
Surface temperature: −241°C (−401.8°F).
Number of moons: 2.

Makemake

Distance from the Sun: minimum 5.7 billion km (3.5 billion miles); maximum 11.8 billion km (7.3 billion miles).
Diameter at the equator: 1,500 km (930 miles).
Time taken to orbit the Sun: 310 Earth years.
Day (single rotation): unknown.
Tilt: 29°.
Surface temperature: −243 to −238°C (−405.4 to −396.4°F).
Number of moons: 0.

Pluto

Distance from the Sun: minimum 4,436 million km (2,750 million miles); maximum 7,375 million km (4,572 million miles).
Diameter at the equator: 2,274 km (1,410 miles).
Time taken to orbit the Sun: 247 Earth years.
Day (single rotation): 6.39 Earth days.
Tilt: 122.5°.
Mass: 0.0022 Earths.
Surface temperature: −220°C (−364°F).
Number of moons: 3, including Charon.

Charon (Pluto's moon)

Distance from Pluto: 19,640 km
(12,177 miles).
Diameter at the equator: 1,192 km
(739 miles).
Time taken to orbit the Sun: 284.54
Earth years.
Day (single rotation): 6.39 Earth days.
Tilt 17°.
Mass: 0.0003 Earths.
Surface temperature: −220°C (−364°F).
Number of moons: 0.

Sedna

Distance from the Sun: minimum 13
billion km (8 billion miles); maximum
150 billion km (93 billion miles).
Diameter at the equator: 1,700 km
(1,054 miles).
Time taken to orbit the Sun: 11.249
Earth years.
Day (single rotation): 10 hours.
Tilt: 11.9°.
Surface temperature: −240°C (−400°F).
Number of moons: 1.

Find out more

Books

The Best Book of the Moon, Ian Graham (Kingfisher/Houghton Mifflin, 2005).

The Creeping Tide, Gail Herman (Kane Press, 2003).

Killer Rocks from Outer Space, Steven Koppes (Lerner Publishing Group, 2004).

The Moon, Carmen Bredeson (Franklin Watts Publishing, 2003).

Stargazers: Could an Asteroid Hit the Earth?, Rosalind Mist (Heinemann Library, 2006).

Turning Points in History: The Moon Landing, Nigel Kelly (Heinemann Library, 2006).

What Do You Think? Is There Other Life In The Universe? Kate Shuster (Heinemann Library, 2009).

Websites

- http://solarsystem.nasa.gov/kids/index.cfm
  Look on NASA's own site for some good activities, such as "Extreme Space", and lots of information about the solar system.

- http://science.nationalgeographic.com/science/space/solar-system
  National Geographic's site is aimed at adults, but is a very accessible and informative run down of how we are exploring the solar system.

- http://www.kidsastronomy.com/solar_system.htm
  Find out more about all the planets and their moons.

- http://www.astronomy.com/asy/default.aspx?c=ss&id=127
  Find out more about the Sun, the Moon, and the planets and how to observe them on this site of Astronomy magazine.

- http://starchild.gsfc.nasa.gov/docs/StarChild/StarChild.html
  Learn all about astronomy and space travel.

- http://www.childrensuniversity.manchester.ac.uk/interactives/science/earthandbeyond/sunrisesunset.asp
  Find out what time the Sun rises and sets on any day of the year.

- http://www.enchantedlearning.com/subjects/astronomy/moon/
  Find out more about the Moon and its phases.

Topics for further study

- Make a sundial. The best way to make a sundial is to find an upright post, such as a post for a clothesline, in a sunny position. Draw a chalk mark on the ground in line with the shadow of the post at midday. The shadow of the post will move round during the day as the spinning of Earth turns it towards, then away from, the Sun. Mark the position of the shadow at each hour of the day. In future, you will be able to tell the time just by looking at the position of the post's shadow.

- Search for life. When the *Viking* lander craft touched down on Mars it tested the Martian surface for life with a test that you can try, too. Take three jars and fill each with sand. Mix two teaspoons of salt into the first jar, two teaspoons of baking powder into the second jar, and two teaspoons of yeast into the third jar. Place the jars in a fridge overnight to mimic the icy Martian night conditions. The next day, pour some sugar into a small jug until it is a quarter full. Top up the jug with warm water, and stir well. Take the jars out of the fridge and pour some sugar water into each one. Leave to stand, noting the changes that occur. After an hour: the jar with the salt will not have reacted at all; the jar with the baking powder will have fizzed a little, then stopped; but the jar with the yeast – the jar with life – will still be bubbling and frothing.

- Get an idea of the scale of the solar system and its planets by making a simple scale model, using different objects to represent each planet and plutoid, Pluto. Represent the four rocky planets and Pluto with peas; Jupiter an orange; Saturn a tangerine; and Uranus and Neptune with two apricots. The Sun can be represented by a beach ball. Using a tape measure, lay out your "planets" using the following distances from "the Sun":

Mercury (pea) 4.4 cm (1.75 in.)	Saturn (tangerine) 1.1 m (3.7 ft)
Venus (pea) 8.25 cm (3.25 in.)	Uranus (apricot) 2.2 m (7.3 ft)
Earth (pea) 11.5 cm (4.5 in.)	Neptune (apricot) 3.4 m (11.4 ft)
Mars (pea) 18 cm (7 in.)	Pluto (pea) 4.5 m (14.7 ft)
Jupiter (orange) 61 cm (24 in.)	

- Observe the Moon. Use a pair of good binoculars to study the Moon on a clear night when the Moon is full. Count how many large craters you can see and how many small ones. Also try to count the dark, flat plains called "seas". You should be able to spot the Tycho crater (near the southern pole) and the Copernicus crater (near the equator, slightly west of the centre). You should also see the Sea of Showers (near the northern pole), the Sea of Serenity (near the equator), and (to the east) the Sea of Tranquility, just south of the Sea of Serenity.

Glossary

asteroid   one of thousands of chunks of rock circling the Sun, mostly between Mars and Jupiter

astronomer   someone who studies outer space, including the planets, stars, and galaxies

atomic clock   world's most accurate clock, timed by the vibrations of atoms

centrifugal force   way things moving in a circle appear to be flung outwards. In fact, "centrifugal force" is not a real force, it is simply their tendency to move in a straight line, not a circle.

chromosphere   middle layer of the Sun's atmosphere, which has a pinkish-red colour

corona   upper atmosphere of the Sun, which consists of a halo of fire and glowing gas

dwarf planet   very small planet, or plutoid

eclipse   event when the light of the Sun is blocked off as the Moon or Earth passes in front of it

equinox   day that occurs twice a year (about 21 March and 21 September) when the midday sun is overhead at the Equator and night and day are 12 hours long all over the world

extrasolar planet   a planet circling a star other than the Sun

gravity   force of attraction between all matter: the force that pulls moons and planets together, and holds the solar system together

inertia   tendency of things to stay still, or keep moving in a straight line, unless forced to do otherwise

lunar   to do with the Moon

map projection   system used to show the round world on a flat map

mass   amount of matter in an object

meteor   shooting star; a small piece of rock that burns up and glows as it enters Earth's atmosphere

meteorite   meteor big enough to survive the journey through Earth's atmosphere and hit the ground

meteoroid   a small body moving in the solar system that would become a meteor if it entered Earth's atmosphere

momentum   degree to which something moving resists stopping. This is similar to inertia.

neap tide   small sea tide that occurs when the Sun and Moon are at right angles to each other

nuclear fusion   joining of the nuclei (cores) of small atoms, such as hydrogen, releasing huge amounts of energy

orbit   path followed by a planet, satellite, or star around a more massive object

orbital resonance   *see* **spin-orbit coupling**

phase   the apparent change in shape of the Moon or a planet as we see it from different angles, and different amounts of its illuminated side are revealed

photosphere   visible surface of the Sun or a star

planet   large round mass circling the Sun or a star

plutoid   dwarf planet further out than Neptune, such as Pluto

retrograde motion   the apparent backward motion of a planet in the night sky as Earth overtakes it

sidereal day   one complete turn of Earth, measured against the distant stars

solar   to do with the Sun

solar flare   enormous explosion looping above the Sun

solar wind   stream of high-energy charged particles blowing out from the Sun

solstice   two days each year (around 21 June and 21 December) when the midday sun is overhead at one of the Tropics, bringing the longest day in one hemisphere and the shortest in the other

spin-orbit coupling   way the rotation of nearby objects in space becomes synchronized

spring tide   extreme sea tide that occurs when the Sun and Moon are aligned

superconducting magnet   electromagnet made extremely powerful by making the coils very conductive in special, very low temperature conditions

weight   force of gravity acting on an object on Earth that pulls it downwards

zenith   highest point reached by the Sun in the sky when it is shining directly at Earth

Index